DATE DUE

How Things Are Made

Beans to Chocolate

By Inez Snyder

Welcome Books™

Children's Press®
A Division of Scholastic Inc.
New York / Toronto / London / Auckland / Sydney
Mexico City / New Delhi / Hong Kong
Danbury, Connecticut

641.3
SNY
c-1
13.95

Thanks to Rose Potts and The Blommer Chocolate Company

Photo Credits: Cover and pp. 7, 9, 11, 13, 15 by Maura B. McConnell; pp. 5, 17 © Owen Franken/Corbis; p. 19 © Richard T. Nowitz/Corbis; p. 21 © James Woolslair/Index Stock Imagery, Inc.
Contributing Editor: Jennifer Silate
Book Design: Mindy Liu

Library of Congress Cataloging-in-Publication Data

Snyder, Inez.
  Beans to chocolate / by Inez Snyder.
  p. cm. — (How things are made)
  Includes index.
  Summary: Follows the process of manufacturing chocolate, from harvesting the cacao beans to making candy.
  ISBN 0-516-24269-5 (lib. bdg.) — ISBN 0-516-24361-6 (pbk.)
  1. Cookery (Chocolate)—Juvenile literature. 2. Chocolate—Juvenile literature. [1. Chocolate.] I. Title. II. Series.

  TX767.C5 S68 2003
  641.3'374—dc21

                                                    2002011306

Contents

Chocolate is made from **cacao beans.**

5

First, the cacao beans are cooked in ovens.

The beans become very hot.

Then, a **machine grinds** the beans.

9

The beans become a **thick** paste.

The paste is mixed with **powdered milk** and sugar.

Machines mix everything together to make chocolate.

The chocolate is very soft.

13

The chocolate cools in pipes.

When the chocolate is cooled, it becomes thicker.

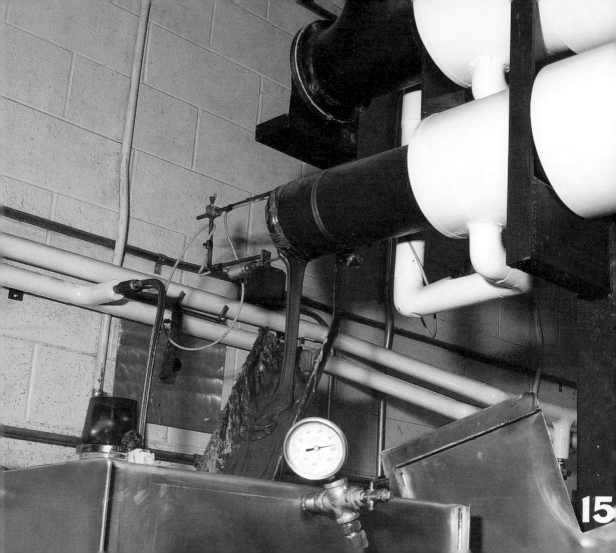

15

Now, the chocolate can be used to make **candy**.

The chocolate is put into **molds** to make candy bars.

The chocolate is cooled in the molds.

As the chocolate cools, it hardens.

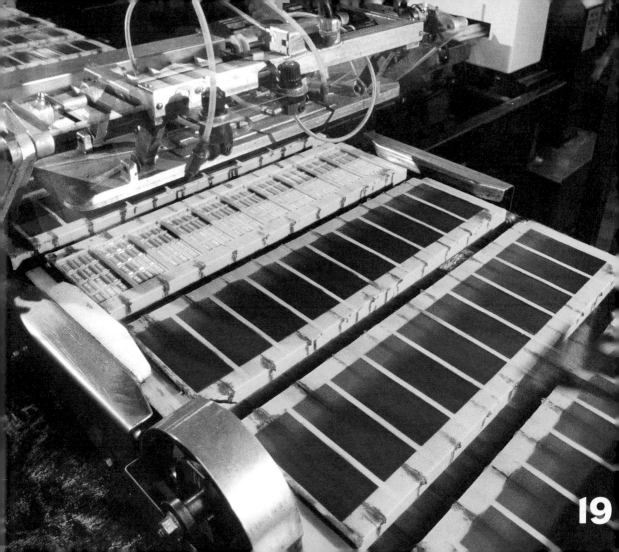
19

Chocolate can be used to make many different kinds of candy.

New Words

cacao beans (kuh-**kaw beenz**) seeds from the cacao tree that are used to make chocolate

candy (**kan**-dee) a sweet food made from sugar

grinds (**grindez**) crushing something into a powder

machine (muh-**sheen**) something that is made to do work or to help make other things

molds (**mohldz**) hollow containers that you can pour liquid into so that it sets in that shape

powdered milk (**poud**-uhrd **milk**) milk that has been dried and made into very tiny pieces

thick (**thik**) not flowing or pouring easily

To Find Out More

Books
Chocolate
by Claire Llewellyn
Children's Press

Vanilla, Chocolate, and Strawberry:
The Story of Your Favorite Flavors
by Bonnie Busenberg
Lerner Publications Company

Web Site
All About Chocolate: Just For Kids
http://www.fmnh.org/Chocolate/kids.html
Learn how chocolate is made and play fun games on this Web site.

Index

About the Author
Inez Snyder writes and edits children's books. She also enjoys painting and cooking for her family.

Reading Consultants
Kris Flynn, Coordinator, Small School District Literacy, The San Diego County Office of Education

Shelly Forys, Certified Reading Recovery Specialist, W.J. Zahnow Elementary School, Waterloo, IL

Sue McAdams, Former President of the North Texas Reading Council of the IRA, and Early Literacy Consultant, Dallas, TX